You can Christmas Scoubidou

VAL MITCHELL AND SELINA COLLINS

CASSELL

Caution: Children must be supervised when using all the materials in this book. Small objects, such as beads and eyes can be choking hazards; scissors and other sharp implements can cause injury; wires and scoubidou strands can be dangerous if flicked or used as tourniquets. Be aware that some of the materials, including some scoubidous, can be flammable and should not be constructed or displayed near naked flames. Confectionery used in the making of some projects must not be eaten.

First published in the United Kingdom by Cassell & Co.

The Orion Publishing Group
5 Upper St Martin's Lane
London WC2H 9EA

Authors: Val Mitchell and Selina Collins
Photography: Val Mitchell and Selina Collins
Design, typesetting and illustration: Steve Hawes
Produced for the Orion Publishing Group by SMPS Ltd, Kedington, Suffolk

A CIP record for this book is available from the British Library

ISBN 0304368199

Printed in the United Kingdom

Contents

★ These pages show simple stitches and projects suitable for beginners and younger children under supervision.

Getting Started

Scoubidou Strands

You may already have caught the scoubidou bug, and if you have, this book will give you lots great ideas to make fantastic festive projects.

There are some easy as well as some more challenging projects for you to choose from and the first-time scoubidouer will learn some simple ways to get started. The book takes you step-by-step through the basic stitches and moves on to some of the more complicated ones. You are shown all the techniques you will need to complete each project.

You will also find some special tips and techniques to help you make your Christmas scoubidous even more exciting.

So, Get Scoubidouing, and have the knottiest Christmas ever!

There are many different makes of scoubidou strands; some are sparkly and see-through, others are in solid colours. You will also find that some strands are thicker than others and it is generally better to use all the same thickness of strands for a project as this makes it easier to keep the stitches even.

Try combining some sparkly strands with some solid colour ones in your projects; you will find that this makes them look glittery as well as brightly coloured.

Other Basic Materials

You will need a few other basic materials to successfully complete the projects in this book and these are as follows:

★ scissors to trim the ends

★ a bradawl to stretch the stitches open so that you can thread through strands and pipe cleaners (you can use a plastic cocktail stick instead of a bradawl, although these break easily so need to be used carefully)

★ a crochet hook to pull through strands and wires

★ glue to stick on eyes and pom poms.

Some projects also use wire:

★ thin jewellery wire for sewing on beads and other items

★ thicker jewellery wire for threading through two or more strands to create larger projects

★ picture wire for making projects that bend.

Craft shops are a good source for most of these materials. Picture wire is available in many DIY shops.

... and Add Some Sparkle!

Adding extra decorations to your Christmas projects can make them look special, so look for lots of different glittery materials to make them really sparkle!

Craft shops are a great place to start. Many sell sparkly pipe cleaners and pom poms and you can also find beads, foiled card and ribbons here. Junk shops are an excellent place to find old necklaces that you can break up for the interesting beads.

Scoubidous can be used to make decorations as well as some really fantastic presents. Sweets can look really effective as bracelets; if you are going to use these you will also need to buy clear varnish to coat them with, otherwise the sweets will go mouldy. Key-rings are good presents for Mums and Dads and are really useful too. You can buy these in key-cutting shops quite cheaply and then decorate them with a scoubidou project.

... and don't forget the pets. Why not make a festive scoubidou for your dog's lead, or make a toy for your cat? Scoubidouing can make Christmas fun for all the family!

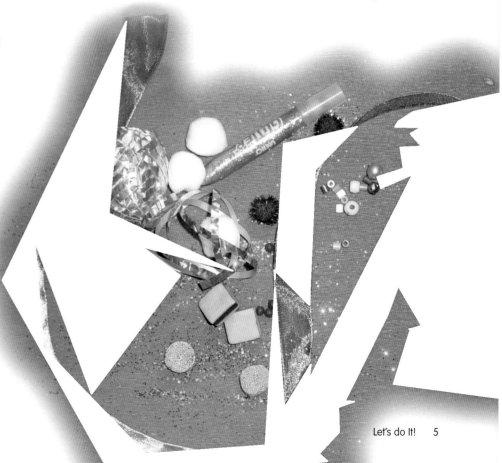

'Off We Go' Stitches

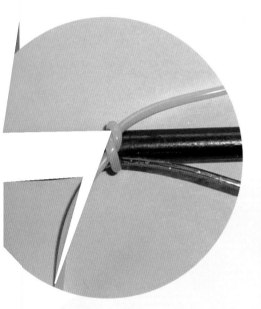

These stitches show you how to begin your projects. If you want to create a bigger loop to attach your final project to, wrap one of your first loops around a pencil like this. Look at the **'Moving On'** section to see the types of designs you can create, beginning with these **'Off We Go'** stitches.

If you are just beginning to scoubidou, start your project off with a simple knot.

'Off We Go' Box Stitch

This stitch can be used to start projects using **'Moving On' Box Stitch** and **'Moving On' Round & Round Stitch**.

a Find the mid-point of each strand and lay strand 3–4 across strand 1–2.

b Bring strand 1 up and loop it over strand 3–4, between strands 2 and 4. Bring strand 2 up and loop it over strand 3–4, between strands 1 and 3.

c Take strand 4 over the loop next to it and under the second loop, into a position between strands 2 and 3 in this diagram.

d Now work in the opposite direction. Take strand 3 over the loop next to it and under the second loop. This should end up in a position between strands 1 and 4 in the diagram.

e Pull the strands together slowly.

f To tighten the stitch up, it is easiest to pull all the strings with equal strength. The final stitch will look a bit like a chessboard pattern.

g The other side of the stitch looks like this.

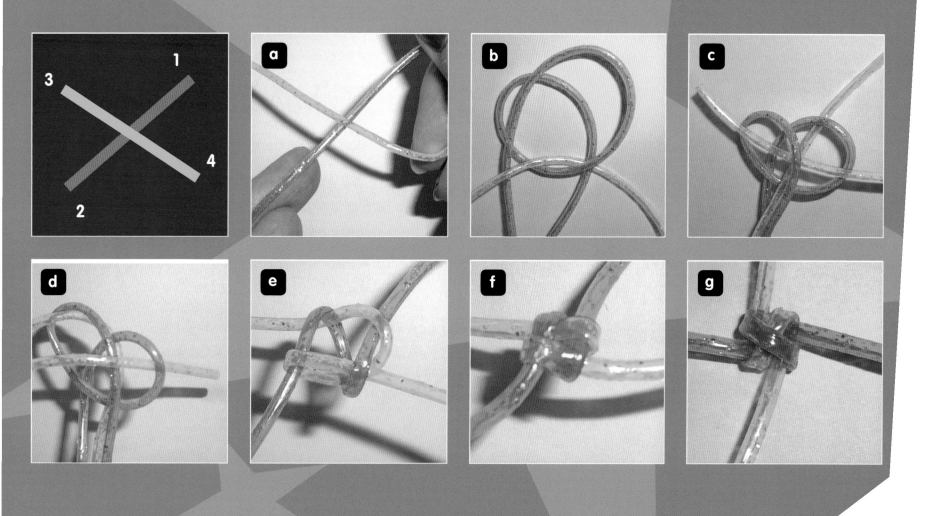

'Off We Go' Stitches

'Off We Go' Wrap It! Stitch

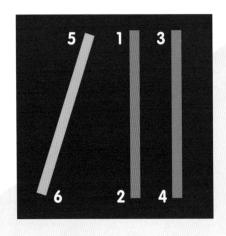

This stitch can be used to start projects using **'Moving On'
Wrap It! Stitch**.

a Take two strands of equal length and make sure the ends
match up together. Tie a granny knot like this.

b Thread strand 5–6 through one loop of the granny knot.

c Pull it through so that the middle of the strand makes a loop
around the knot strand.

Pull the knot tight.

d Take strand 4 over strands 5 and 6, then under strand 2.

e Take strand 2 under strands 5 and 6, then out through the loop
made by strand 4.

f Pull the knot tight like this.

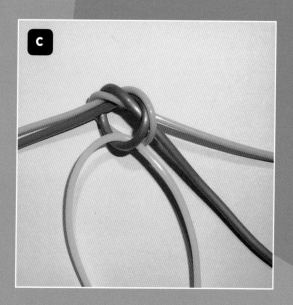

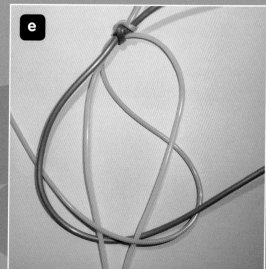

'Off We Go' Stitches

'Off We Go' 1, 2, 3 Stitch

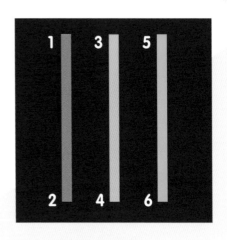

This stitch can be used to start projects using **'Moving On' 1, 2, 3 Stitch**.

a Tie a granny knot in all three strings to secure ends 1, 3 and 5.

b Separate out the long strands (2, 4 and 6).

c Take strand 2 over strand 4 and hold to make a loop.

d Now pass strand 4 over strand 6 and hold to make a second loop.

e Take strand 6 and pass it through the loop you made with strand 2.

f Pull the strands slowly with the same strength in opposite directions to make the stitch.

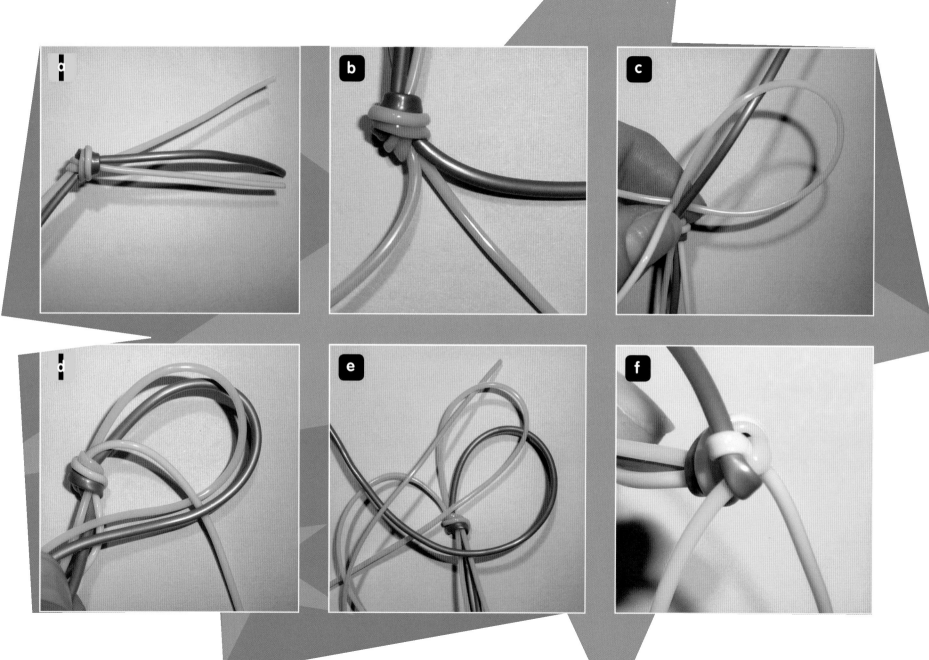

'Off We Go' Stitches

'Off We Go'
Over & Under Stitch

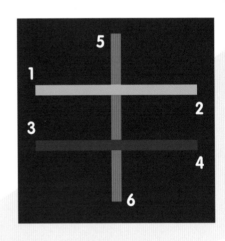

This stitch can be used to start projects using **'Moving On' Over & Under Stitch** and **'Moving On' Do the Twist! Stitch**.

a Lay strands 1–2 and 3–4 over strand 5–6.

b Pass strand 5 over the centre strands, and make a loop between strands 3 and 6. Then pass strand 6 over the centre strands and make a loop between strands 5 and 2.

c Take strand 2 (working right to left) over the loop next to it and under the second loop. Take strand 1 (working left to right) over the loop next to it and under the second loop.

d Take strand 4 (working right to left) over the loop next to it and under the second loop.

e Take strand 3 (working left to right) over the loop next to it and under the second loop.

f Pull the strands slowly, with the same strength, in opposite directions to make the stitch.

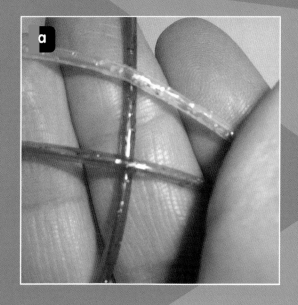

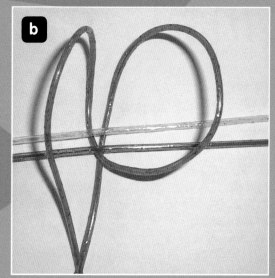

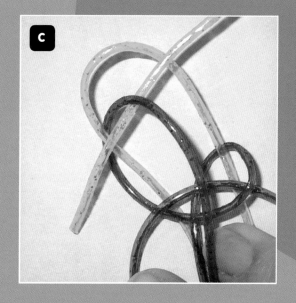

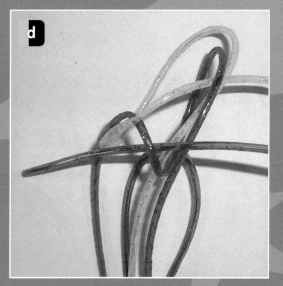

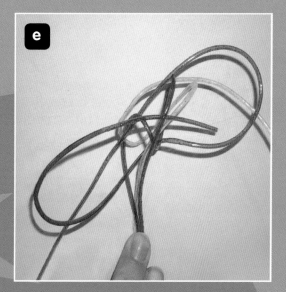

'Moving On' Stitches

These stitches show you how to create the main part of your project. Try changing stitches like **'Moving On' Box Stitch** and **'Moving On' Round & Round Stitch** part way through a project to see what happens!

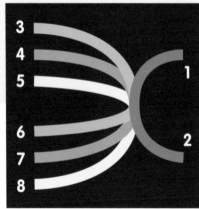

'Moving On' Weaving Stitch

This is a good stitch for first-time scoubidouers as it gives you practice in weaving strands over and under. It is really excellent for making bracelets and bookmarks!

You will need four strands (in different colours) for this stitch.

a Find the centre of the four strands and tie a knot.

b Separate out two same-colour strands (strands 1 and 2) from the rest and splay out the other six strands (strands 3–8) so that there is one of each colour on each side of the knot. The colours should be arranged in the same order on each side.

c You are now ready to weave! Take strand 1 and thread over strand 3, under strand 4 and then alternately over and under strands 5–8 until you come out the other side.

d The next step is to follow the same process in the other direction using strand 2: thread this strand over strand 8, under strand 7 and then alternately over and under strands 6–3 until you come out the other side.

e Continue the process in points **d** and **e** until you have completed the project, making sure you have left at least 6cm of each strand free at the end.

f Weaving stitch can be finished off with a simple knot (turn to page 36 to find out more about finishing off projects).

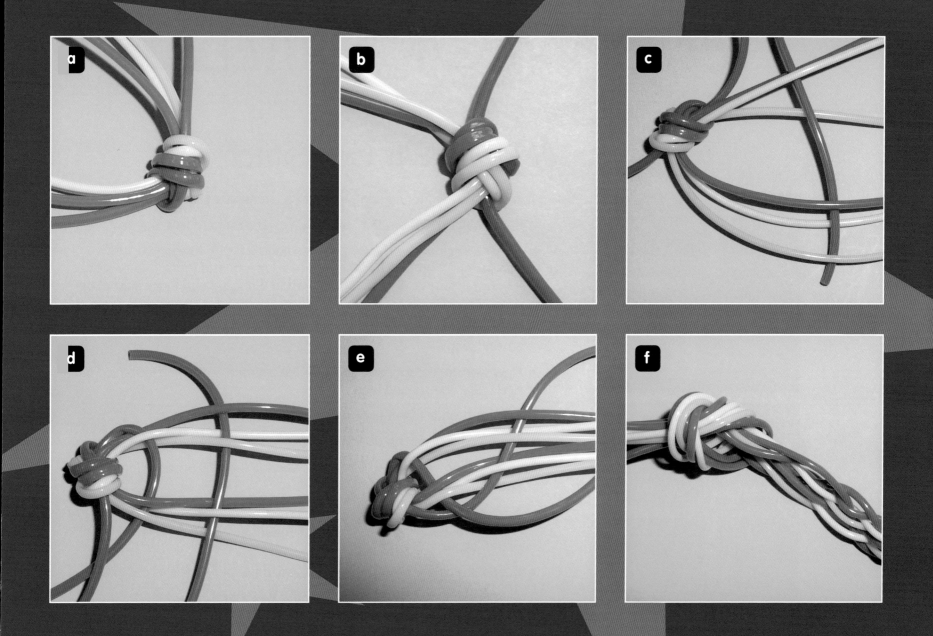

'Moving On' Stitches

'Moving On' Box Stitch

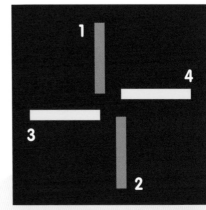

This stitch is good for creating tree candy, snowflakes and Christmas trees.

a Begin with an **'Off We Go' Box Stitch** as shown here (see pages 6–7).

b Turn the work over, so you have the 'diagonal' side facing you, and bring strand 1 up (black in the picture – top left) and make a loop with it between strands 2 and 3. Bring strand 2 (the second black strand) up and make a loop with it between strands 1 and 4.

c Take strand 4, working right to left, over the loop next to it and under the second loop.

d Now work in the opposite direction. Take strand 3 over the loop next to it and under the second loop.

e Pull the strands together slowly and tighten the stitch up.

f For the next stitch, the direction reverses (see diagram bottom left).

Make a loop with strand 1 between strands 2 and 4; make a loop with strand 2 between strands 1 and 3.

Now, working left to right, pass strand 3 over the first loop and under the second. Finally, take strand 4 (working right to left) over the first loop and under the second.

g Keep alternating the stitches in this way until your project is complete.

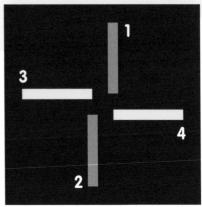

Turn to page 32 to see how to finish off a **Box Stitch** project.

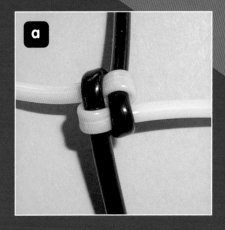

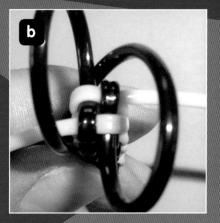

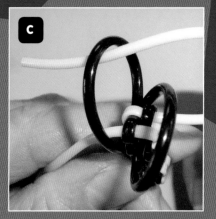

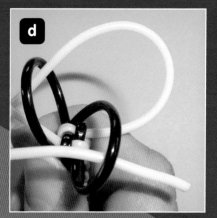

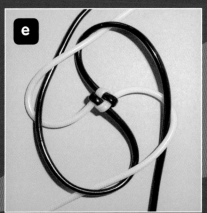

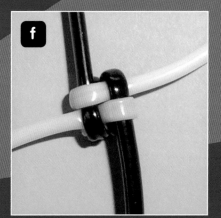

'Moving On' Stitches

'Moving On' Wrap It! Stitch

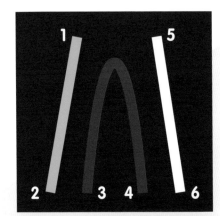

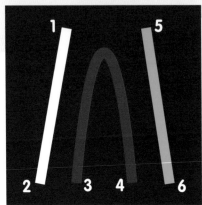

This stitch is good for creating headbands and reindeer tails.

a Begin with an **'Off We Go' Wrap It! Stitch** as shown here (see pages 8–9).

Take strand 2 (the blue strand in the picture) across the front of strands 3 and 4.

b Bring strand 6 (white in this picture) over the top of strand 2, passing it under strands 3 and 4, before ...

c ... finally threading it through the loop made by strand 2.

d For the next stitch, the direction reverses (diagram left, below).

Take strand 6 (the blue strand in the picture on the right) across the front of strands 3 and 4.

e Bring strand 2 (white) over the top of strand 6, passing it under strands 3 and 4, before finally threading it through the loop made by strand 6.

f Keep alternating the stitches in this way until your project is complete.

Finish off your project with some sparkly beads and fancy knots (see page 36).

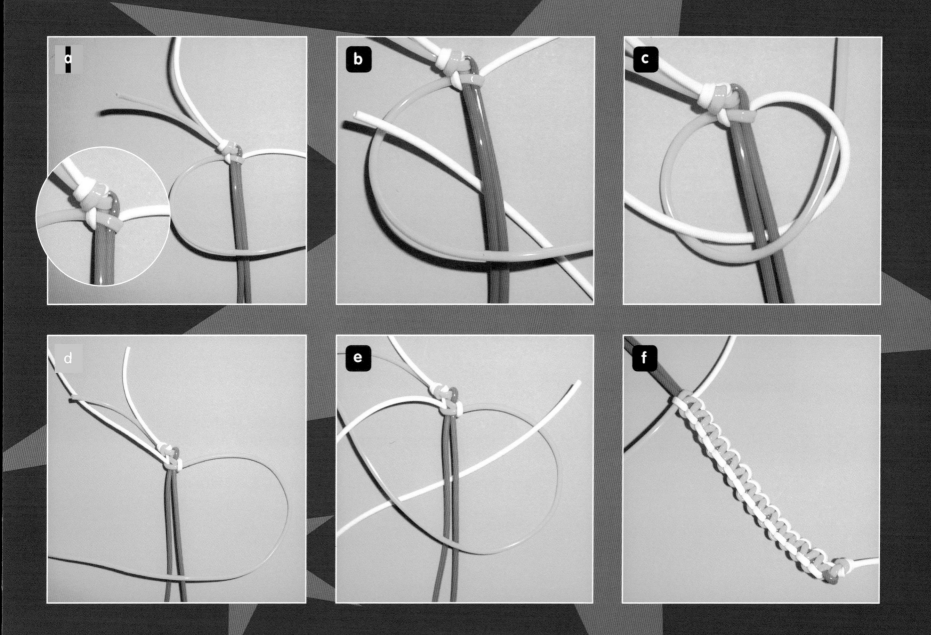

'Moving On' Stitches

'Moving On' 1, 2, 3 Stitch

This stitch is good for creating key-rings and animal legs.

a Begin with an **'Off We Go' 1, 2, 3 Stitch** (see pages 10–11).

Take strand 1 (black in this picture) over strand 2 (turquoise in this picture).

b Now take strand 2 around strand 1 (see picture) and over strand 3.

c Pass strand 3 around strand 2 (in the same way as you did with strand 2 in step b) and through the loop made by strand 1.

d Pull the stitch tight.

e Turn the project around so that the coloured strands are all in the position they started at and repeat until your project is finished.

Turn to page 32 to see how to finish off a **1, 2, 3 Stitch** project.

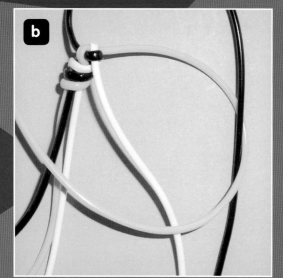

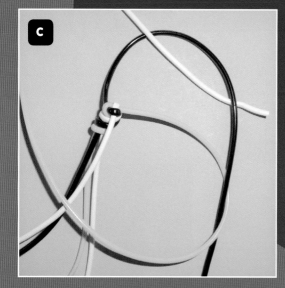

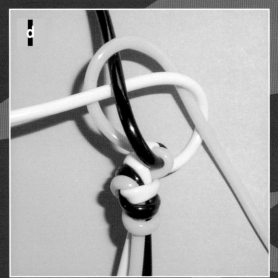

'Moving On' Stitches

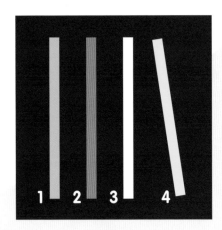

'Moving On' Helter Skelter Stitch

This stitch is good for creating headbands and Christingle oranges.

You will need four strands to do this stitch.

a Begin this stitch with a granny knot (see right).

b Pass strand 4 over the other three strands …

c … then behind them and up through the loop you have just made.

d Pull the strands tight and continue with the stitch until you have completed your project.

e Now untie the granny knot you made at the beginning and follow the instructions for **Wrap It! Stitch** (see page 18).

f Turn to page 32 to find out how to finish off your project with **Box Stitch**.

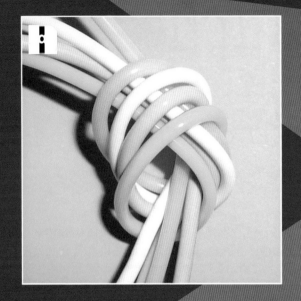

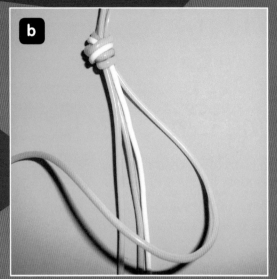

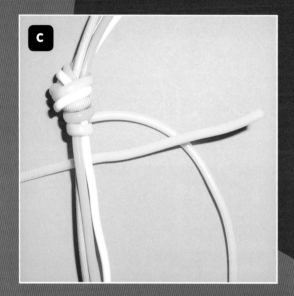

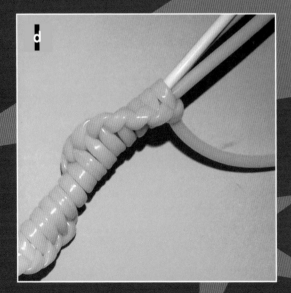

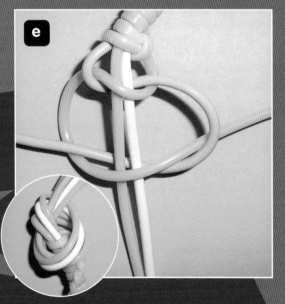

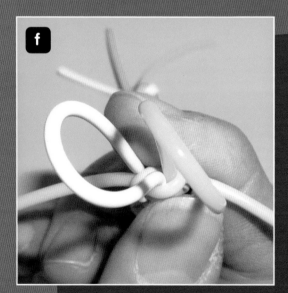

'Moving On' Stitches

'Moving On' Over & Under Stitch

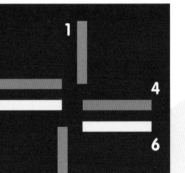

This stitch is great for creating bracelets as well as reindeer heads and bodies.

a Begin with an **'Off We Go' Over & Under Stitch** as shown here (see pages 12–13).

Begin with the black strands (1 and 2 in the diagram, top left). Loop strand 1 over strands 4 and 6 to end up between strands 2 and 6. Loop strand 2 over strands 3 and 5 to end up between strands 1 and 3.

b Now take strand 3 (pink in this case), working from left to right, over the first loop and under the second.

Working right to left, take the same colour strand (4) over the first loop and under the second.

c You are now going to work with the final colour. Working from left to right, take strand 5 over the first loop and under the second loop.

d Finally, working from right to left, take strand 6 over the first loop and under the second loop.

e Pull the strands together slowly to make the stitch.

f For the next stitch, the direction reverses (see diagram, bottom left). Begin with the black strands again (1 and 2 in this picture). Loop strand 1 over strands 3 and 5 to end up between strands 2 and 5. Loop strand 2 over strands 4 and 6 to end up between strands 1 and 4.

g Now take strand 4 (pink in this case), working from right to left, over the first loop and under the second. Working with the remaining same colour strand (3), thread this left to right over the first loop and under the second.

h Now for the final colour. Working from right to left, take strand 6 over the first loop and under the second loop. Then, working from left to right, take strand 5 over the first loop and under the second loop, pulling the strands tightly to make the stitch.

Turn to page 34 to see how to finish off an **Over & Under Stitch** project.

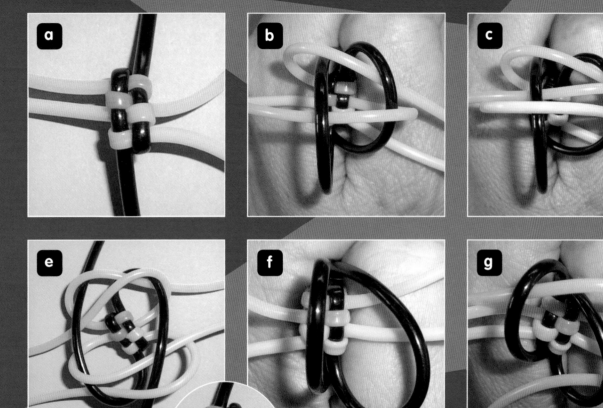

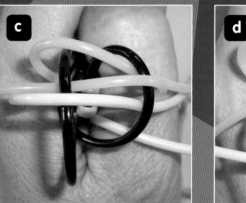

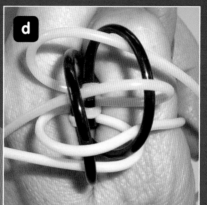

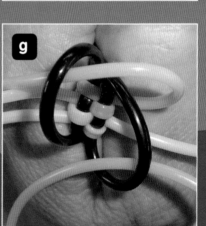

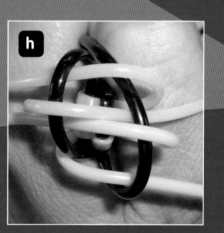

'Moving On' Round & Round Stitch

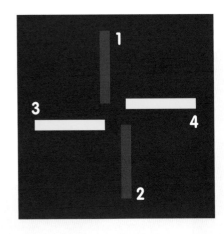

This stitch is good for creating robin legs.

a Begin this stitch with an **'Off We Go' Box Stitch** (see pages 6–7).

Pass strand 1 diagonally across the checker pattern and between strands 2 and 4 to form a loop.

b Pass strand 2 diagonally across the checker pattern and between strands 1 and 3 to form a second loop.

c Pass strand 3 (working from left to right) over the first loop and under the second loop.

d Pass strand 4 (working from right to left) over the first loop and under the second loop.

e Pull the stitch tight and …

f … continue with your project until it is completed.

Turn to page 32 to see how to finish off a **Round & Round Stitch** project with **Box Stitch**.

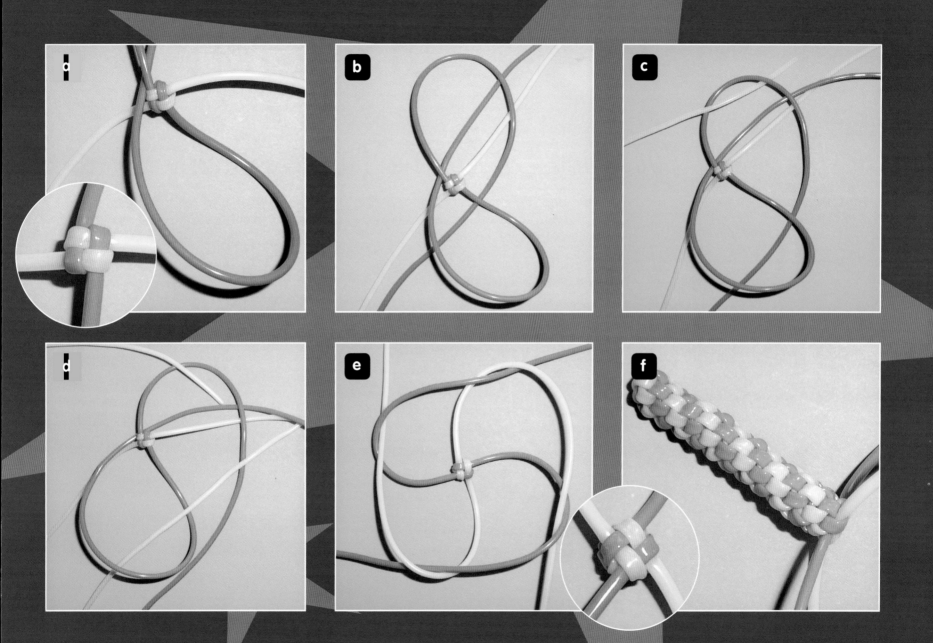

'Moving On' Do the Twist! Stitch

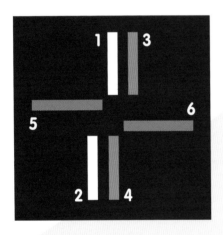

This stitch is good for creating bracelets and wreaths. The parcel sweets on page 62 use an advanced version of this stitch.

a Begin this stitch with an **'Off We Go' Over & Under Stitch** (see pages 12–13).

Pass strand 1 over strand 5 to make a loop between strands 5 and 2.

b Pass strand 2 (the second white strand here) over to make a loop between strands 1 and 3.

c Now strand 3 creates a loop by passing between strands 2 and 4.

d The final strand (strand 4) passes between strands 3 and 6 to make a fourth loop.

e You can now begin to thread. Take strand 6 and thread it over the first loop, under the second loop. Continue to thread over the third loop and under the fourth.

f Now, working from left to right, do the same with strand 5: thread it over the first loop and under the second; over the third loop and under the fourth.

g Pull the stitch together slowly, taking strands 1, 3 and 6 in one hand; 5, 2 and 4 in the other.

h Begin the next stitch exactly as for the first and continue until you have completed your project.

Follow the instructions on page 34 to finish your project with the **Over & Under Stitch** method.

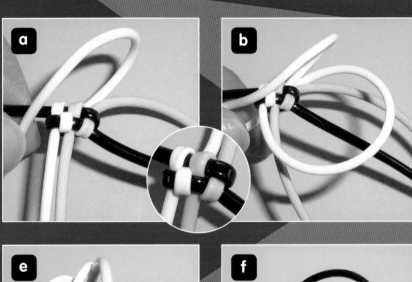

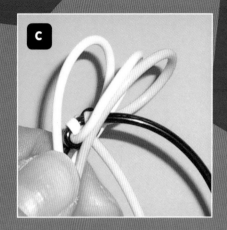

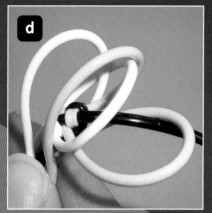

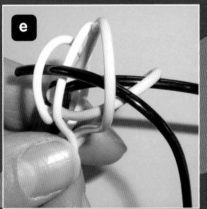

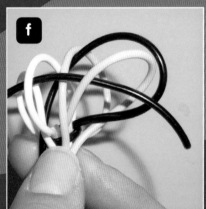

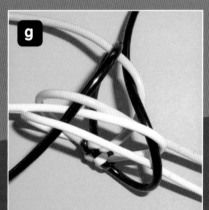

'Moving On' Stitches

'Moving On' ... and Joining Up

Sometimes you may need more than one length of scoubidou to make the bigger projects, or you may wish to change direction!

We show three methods for joining strands here.

Staggered joins

This join works well for **'Moving On': Box Stitch**; **1, 2, 3 Stitch**; **Over & Under Stitch**; **Round & Round Stitch** and **Do the Twist! Stitch**.

a Make sure the ends of your scoubidou strands are trimmed to different lengths so that you do not make a join more than every three stitches.

Thread in a new strand from the opposite direction and parallel to the strand you are finishing off, like this.

Continue with the next stitch, using the strand you are finishing off.

Pull this very tightly to secure the new strand.

b You can now begin to work with the new strand. Cut the old strand close to the project after you have completed two more stitches.

Wired joins

This join works well for **'Moving On': Wrap It! Stitch** and **Helter Skelter Stitch**.

It is important to join the strands for these stitches before you begin, otherwise the strands will pull apart.

c Thread a length of jewellery wire through both strands you are intending to join, leaving about 8cm poking out of each end.

When you come close to the join, you will need to hold the wire at the free end of the second strand so that, as you go over the gap, the two strands are pushed together.

Double joins

This joins can be done with **'Moving On': Box Stitch**; **Over & Under Stitch**; **Round & Round Stitch** and **Do the Twist! Stitch**.

Try using the double join to add legs to animals and make snowflakes.

d Create your two sections to the required length.

Put the two working ends of the project together, you will now begin to work sideways.

Using two (or three for **Over & Under Stitch** and **Do the Twist! Stitch**) strands from each side, continue to create stitches like this.

e Follow exactly the same process on the opposite side of the project …

f … and you will then have a neat square hole in the middle.

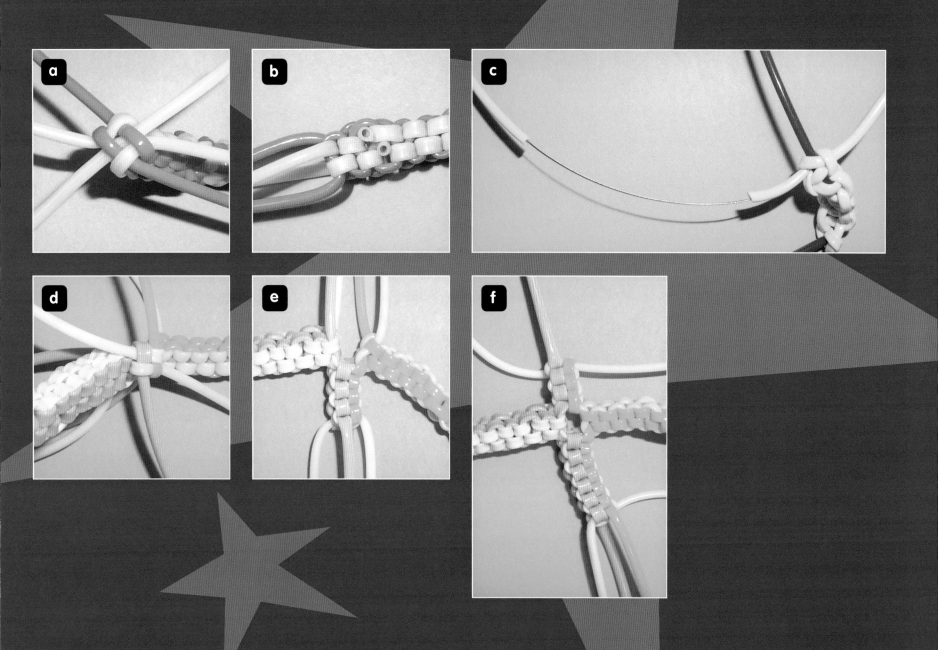

'Time to Stop' Stitches

The basic finishing off stitches are shown on the next few pages. If you want to make your projects look even more festive, try some of the ideas shown on pages 36–37.

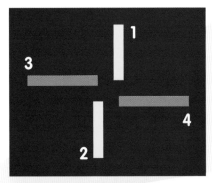

'Time to Stop' Box Stitch

Take your **Box Stitch** or **Round & Round Stitch** project and…

a Create a **'Moving On' Box Stitch**, leaving it loose like this.

b Look at the diagram top left. Take strand 2 under strand 4 and up through the middle of the **Box Stitch**.

c Now take strand 4 under strand 1 and up through the middle of the **Box Stitch**.

d Keep working anti-clockwise. Take strand 1 under strand 3, passing this up through the middle of the **Box Stitch**.

e Finally, pass strand 3 under the loop created by strand 2 in step **b**, and up through the middle of the **Box Stitch** so that all four strands are pointing in the same direction.

f Pull the strands evenly and tightly to created a rounded end, like this.

'Time to Stop' 1, 2, 3 Stitch

Take your **1, 2, 3 Stitch** project and…

g Create a **'Moving On' 1, 2, 3 Stitch**, leaving it loose like this.

h Look at the diagram bottom left. Working anti-clockwise as you did for the **Box Stitch**, take strand 1 under strand 3 and up through the middle of the **1, 2, 3 Stitch**.

i Take strand 3 under strand 2 and up through the middle of the **1, 2, 3 Stitch**.

j Finally, take strand 2 under the loop created by strand 1 in step **b**, and up through the middle of the **1, 2, 3 Stitch** so that all three strands are pointing in the same direction.

k Pull the strands evenly and tightly …

l … to create a rounded end, like this.

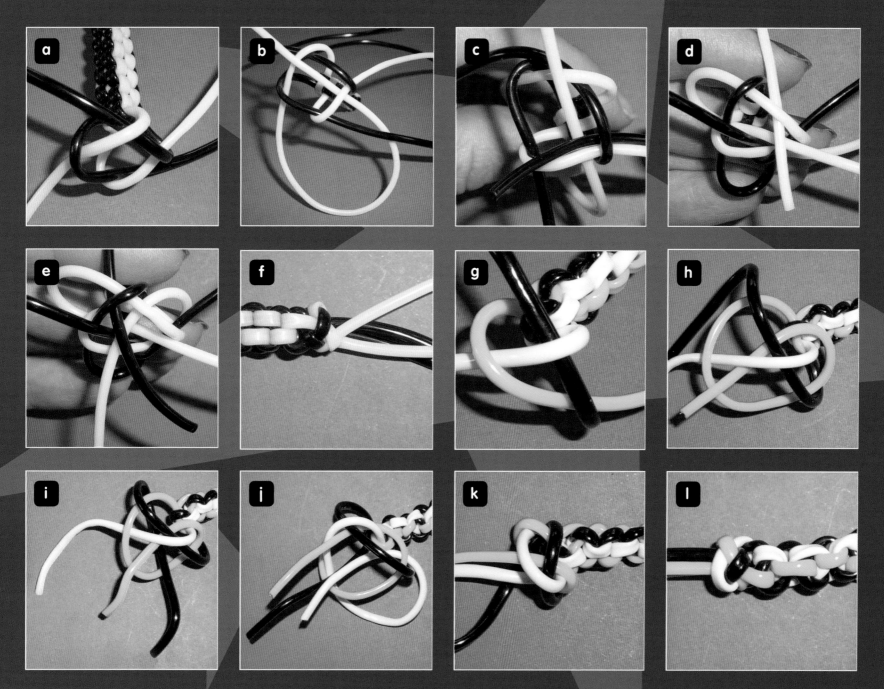

'Time to Stop' Stitches

'Time to Stop' Over & Under Stitch

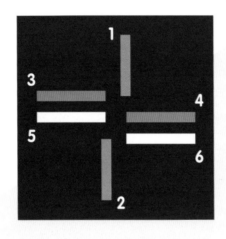

Take your **Over & Under Stitch** or **Do the Twist! Stitch** project and…

a Create a **'Moving On' Over & Under Stitch**, leaving it loose like this.

b Take strand 1 under strand 3 and up through the upper hole (made by strands 3 and 4) in the middle of the **Over & Under Stitch**.

c Now take strand 3 under strand 5 and up through the lower hole (made by strands 5 and 6) in the middle of the **Over & Under Stitch**.

d Keep working anti-clockwise. Take strand 5 under strand 2, passing this up through the middle of the lower hole.

e Take strand 2 under strand 6, passing this strand up through the middle of the lower hole. You now have three strands through the middle of the lower hole and one through the upper hole.

Now pass strand 6 under strand 4 and up through the middle of the upper hole.

f Finally, pass strand 4 under the loop created under strand 1 and up through the middle of the upper hole. There are now three strands coming through each of the two holes.

g Pull the strands evenly and tightly to created a rounded end, like this.

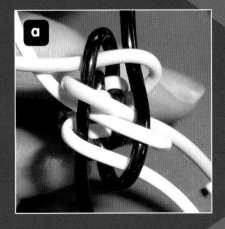

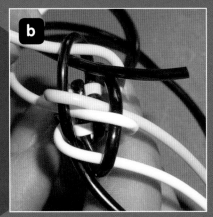

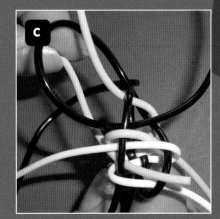

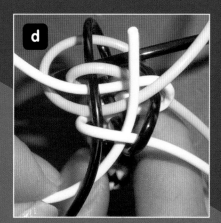

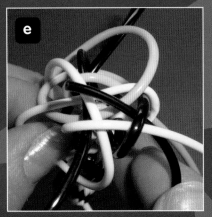

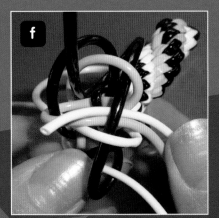

'Time to Stop' Stitches

Trim it Up!

One of the easiest ways to make your projects look Christmassy is to finish them off with beads and sparkly trimmings. Here are a few ideas to get you started...

Knots and tassels

Nearly all scoubidou projects can be finished off with knots.

a Tieing a simple knot or a number of knots works well for bracelets.

b Adding ribbon tied through a knot can make a bracelet present look really special.

Beads

Beads can be used to decorate your projects and to represent berries or eyes.

c Glass beads work well on Christmas decorations as they shine in the light. This decoration was threaded with picture wire and the beads slipped onto the ends. The wire was then twisted to secure them.

d Two beads were threaded onto the strands of this snake bracelet before the ends were knotted to make a tongue. Notice how the ends of the strands are cut at an angle to make the tongue look forked.

e The beads on the end of this decoration make good yellow berries. They are secured by threading thin scoubidou strands through the centre of the beads before knotting off the strands.

Christmas trimmings

Shiny decorations look good at Christmas when they catch the light and by using sparkly pom poms and pipe cleaners in your Christmas scoubidou projects, you can make them twinkle too!

f You can feed sparkly pom poms onto scoubidou strands by inserting a needle into your strand and pushing the other end through the pom pom like this. You can also wire them on with picture wire.

g Sparkly pipe cleaners can be used to hang up projects and also secure the ends of them. This string of Christmas candles is decorated with a sparkly pipe cleaner and also helps it to be bent into shape.

h White pom poms are useful for finishing off baubles and other projects to give them a snowy look!

Let's Get Festive!

Anna's Christmas Headband

With Christmas comes the party season and scoubidou headbands can look fantastic with your party gear, just look for ways to trim them up with ribbons or pom poms. This headband is easy to make and looks pretty good too! 'Moving On' Wrap It! Stitch works just as well for this project.

★ You will need: four different coloured scoubidou strands; a headband to wrap the strands around; 0.5m of ribbon to trim.

a Tie a knot about 6cm from the end of all four strands and pull tight around the end of the headband.

b Choose one colour and begin **'Moving On' Helter Skelter Stitch** around all the other strands as well as the headband. Create five stitches.

c Next, use the strand closest to the end of this last stitch and continue with **'Moving On' Helter Skelter Stitch** until you have gone completely round the headband; you will need to do between eight and twelve stitches, depending on the thickness of the band and the strands. Choose another different colour strand and do another complete turn of the headband.

d Continue with **'Moving On' Helter Skelter Stitch**, changing the colours as described in point **c** until you are 3cm from the end of the shortest strand. Pull this last stitch really tight.

e Now find the centre of your piece of ribbon and wind it around the headband, over the end of the strands and down to cover the remaining undecorated section of the headband.

f Complete the headband by finishing off with a bow.

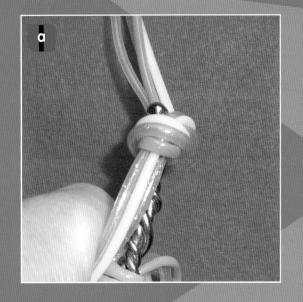

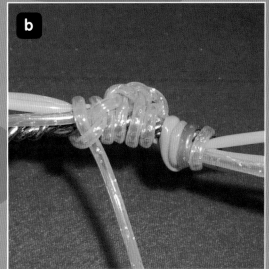

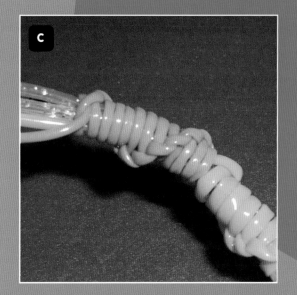

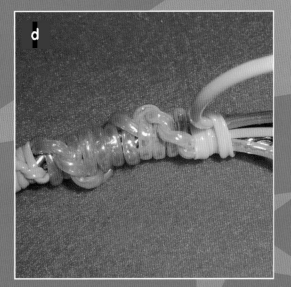

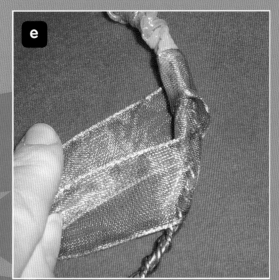

Let's Get Festive!

Cards Galore!

Impress your parents and friends by making these simple and effective paperclip Christmas cards. You can make many different designs using this technique, here we show you how to make the mistletoe card.

★ You will need: one green scoubidou strand; two paper clips, a white bead; a round template (such as a coffee jar lid), glue and glitter to decorate your card.

a Cut the green scoubidou strand into three equal pieces and knot the end of one piece around the narrow end of a paperclip.

b Thread the strand under one side of the paperclip and across like this. Pull tight.

c Now work the other way, threading the strand under the side of the paperclip where the strand is now sitting, through the middle and out the other side.

d Repeat points **b** and **c** until you have covered the whole length of the paperclip, you will just have a semi-circular piece of metal showing. To cover this, keep looping the strand around the base and knot the final loop.

e Make another paperclip leaf exactly the same as this first one. You are now going to join them together. Feed the strands from the narrow ends of the paperclips through a bead and knot together tightly. Trim the end of one strand close to the knot to leave one 'twig'.

f To make the card, fold a piece of stiff card in half and draw a circle around a lid with a pencil (or gold pen) to create a frame for your mistletoe design.

g Use glue and glitter to decorate your card and pierce a hole in the centre of the design large enough to thread two scoubidou strands through.

h Thread both ends of the remaining piece of green scoubidou strand through the hole and put your mistletoe through the loop you have created; the loop should fit between the 'berry' and the two 'leaves'. Pull tight at the back of the card and knot to secure the mistletoe.

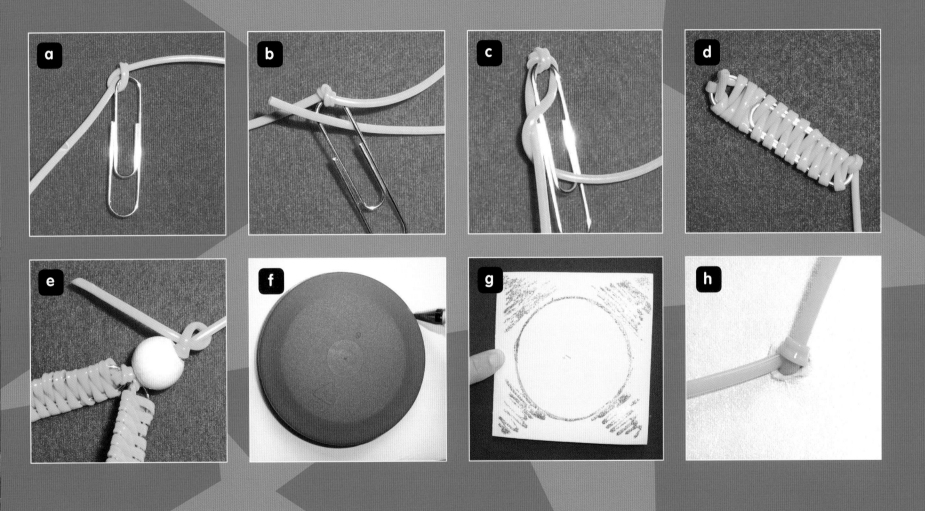

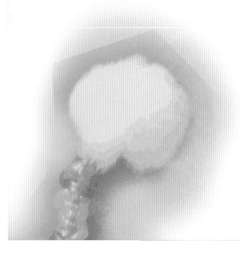

Let's Get Festive!

Santa's Stockings Card-holder

Show off your favourite Christmas cards with these lovely stocking card-holders. This is a great project to start you off, as the more quirky your stocking shapes are, the more realistic the look!

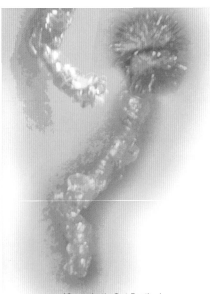

★ You will need: one scoubidou strand for hanging the cards on; two scoubidou strands (in different colours) for each stocking; small clothes pegs; pom poms and wire for decorating the stockings.

a Find the centre of the two scoubidou strands you have chosen for your stocking and tie a knot.

b Using one of the strands from the top of the knot, create a **'Moving On' Helter Skelter Stitch** around the other three strands and pull tight. This is the top of your stocking.

c Using the same strand, create three more **'Moving On' Helter Skelter Stitches**. Swap to the second colour, using the strand nearest to the end of the last knot.

d Create another three **'Moving On' Helter Skelter Stitches** (as you did in point **c** and swap the colours again, creating another four stitches one more time. Now create two **'Moving On' Box Stitches** to make the heel.

e Next, alternate the colours again, using **'Moving On' Helter Skelter Stitch** to create the foot of the sock.

f Finish off the end of the foot with a **'Time to Stop' Box Stitch** and pull the strands tight.

g Decorate the top of the sock with a pom pom, using a small piece of wire or cotton to tie it around one of the strands at the top of the sock.

You can make this project any length. Create as many socks as you like (in any colours), then thread these onto a ribbon or scoubidou strand, alternating the socks with tiny clothes pegs.

You can now clip on your Christmas cards and hang the project up.

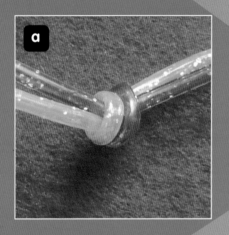

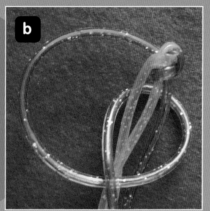

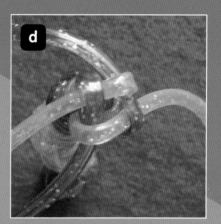

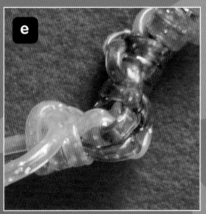

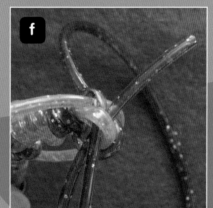

Let's Get Festive!

Tree Candy

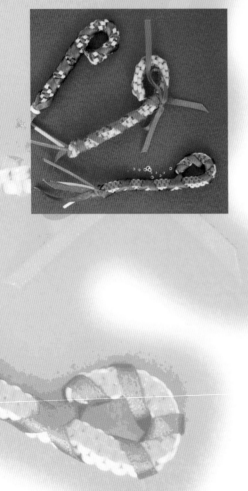

These little candy sticks are one of the easiest Christmas projects to make, as they use just one stitch. They can be made with either Box Stitch or Round and Round Stitch. We have used Box Stitch here.

★ You will need: two scoubidou strands in different colours; medium gauge jewellery wire to thread through the strands; narrow ribbon to wind around the final candy (optional).

a Thread the jewellery wire through each of the strands, leaving about 6cm of wire sticking out from each of the four ends.

b Begin with an **'Off We Go' Box Stitch**, being careful to make sure you start in the middle of the two strands.

c Continue with **'Moving On' Box Stitch** like this.

d Carry on creating the project with **Box Stitch**, keeping the shape as straight as you can, until you get to 4cm from the end of the strands.

e Finish off neatly with a **'Time to Stop' Box Stitch** and pull the strands tight.

f Trim the ends off these strands to finish off the bottom of the candy stick; they can look good if you cut them at an angle.

g Thread wire through the **'Off We Go' Box Stitch** you began the project with, and then through the main stem of the candy to make a 'handle'. Decorate with ribbon (a crochet hook is useful for pulling the ribbons through the stitch at the base of the candy stick).

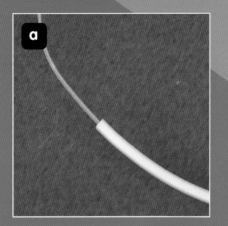

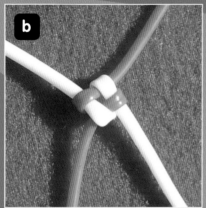

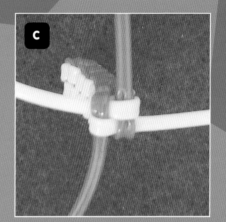

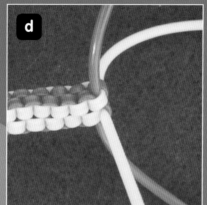

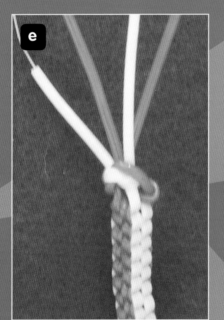

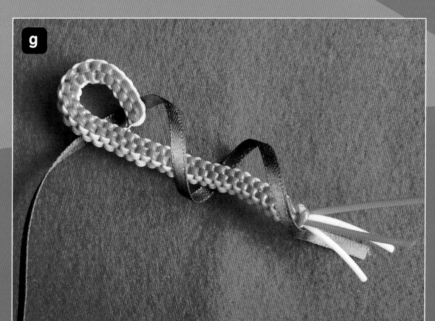

Let's Get Festive!

Falling Flakes

Sparkling snowflakes can be hung on holy twigs for a frosty festive look; they also work well on a Christmas mobile. Adding sparkly pipe cleaners in similar or contrasting colours make the snowflakes twinkle in the light!

★ You will need: six scoubidou strands, all the same colour; two sparkly pipe cleaners, each cut into two equal lengths; ribbon to hang the snowflake up (optional).

a Begin with an **'Off We Go' Box Stitch**, being careful to make sure you start in the middle of the two strands. Continue with **'Moving On' Box Stitch** until the project is 3.5cm long.

b Now create another identical project and put two adjacent strands from each project together, like this.

c Create a **'Moving On' Box Stitch** with these four strands and it pull tight. You have now begun another branch of the snowflake.

d Continue with **'Moving On' Box Stitch** until the project is 2cm long. Now create a final branch (as explained in point **a**) and join this to a branch of the main project (as explained in points **c** and **d**).

e Join up the last four free ends to complete the snowflake shape.

f Finish off two of the 2cm branches with **'Time to Stop' Box Stitch**.

g With the final branch, pull the last stitch tight, and cut two opposite strands close to the project. The final two strands are tied to make the hanger.

h Finally, thread the sparkly pipe cleaners through the centre hole to make additional branches.

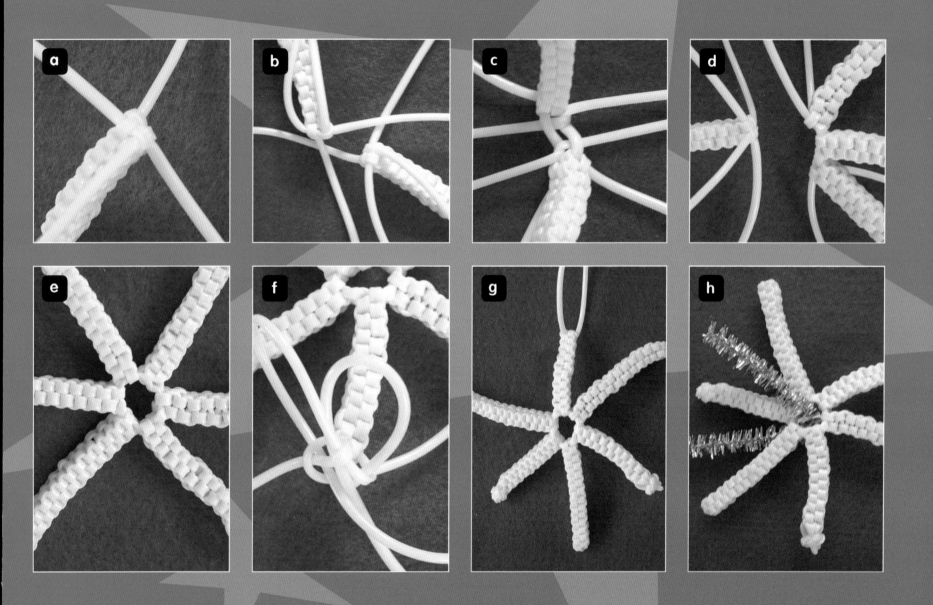

Let's Get Festive!

Christingle Oranges

These festive oranges are made at the beginning of advent. The Christingle orange represents the world, the candle on top is to show light and hope, and the red around the centre indicates sacrifice.

★ You will need: one white and one yellow scoubidou strand to make the candle; one yellow and two red scoubidou strands to make the centre spiral; an orange; cocktail sticks and sweets for decoration; a small container (such as a tealight holder to stand the orange up).

To make the candle

a Begin with an **'Off We Go' Box Stitch**, being careful to make sure you start in the middle of the two strands.

b Continue with **'Moving On' Box Stitch** until the project is 3cm long.

c Find a yellow or red bead and wire onto the top to make a flame.

d Loop the loose ends around the orange, spreading the strands out evenly. Tie in a knot underneath and trim off the ends.

To make the band

e Fold the yellow strand in half and use the red strand to create **'Moving On' Helter Skelter Stitch**.

f Continue until you have about 6cm left at the end of the red strand and knot the next red strand to the end of this. Pull tightly and trim the ends.

g Continue with **'Moving On' Helter Skelter Stitch** until the project is long enough to fit around the waist of the orange. Now tie the two free yellow ends to the loop you made at the beginning.

h Continue with **'Moving On' Helter Skelter Stitch** to cover the yellow joins, knotting the end around one of the first **'Moving On' Helter Skelter Stitches**. Trim and fit over the orange.

Finally, decorate the orange with cocktail sticks and sweets.

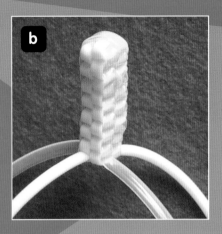

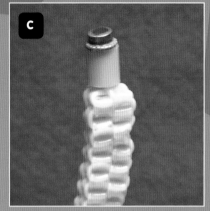

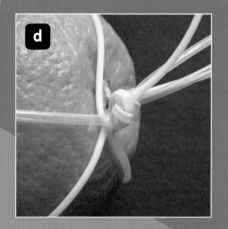

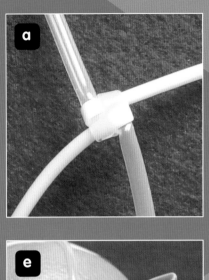

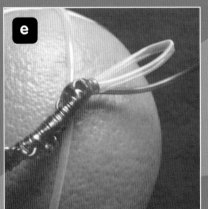

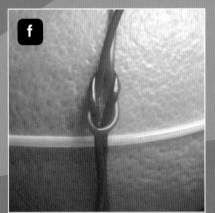

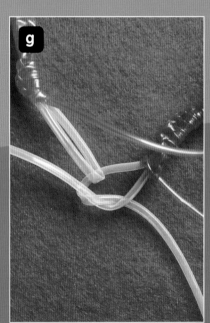

Let's Get Festive!

Sparkling Christmas Trees

These trees are easy to make and work best if you pick a colour theme. They look really festive if you use a mixture of plain and sparkly scoubidou strands and shiny pipe cleaners for the branches.

★ You will need: two scoubidou strands for the main stem; four scoubidou strands (at least two different colours) for the branches, each cut into eight equal pieces; two sparkly pipe cleaners cut to same length as the strands (optional); base for the tree such as a cotton reel covered in silver foil.

a Begin with an **'Off We Go' Box Stitch** followed by eight **'Moving On' Box Stitches**. Now create a new **'Moving On' Box Stitch** and leave it loose.

b Thread two of the short strand 'branches' you have made through the loose **Box Stitch** until the branches are of equal length on each side of the stitch.

c Pull the strands tight.

d Create another **'Moving On' Box Stitch** and thread one pipe cleaner branch through, but at a right angle to the first branches, pulling the strands tight again.

e Continue like this, creating **Moving On' Box Stitches**, and threading pairs of strands through, each time at right angles to the previous pair. Repeat this four times before adding another pipe cleaner branch.

Keep repeating this pattern with four sets of strands and one pipe cleaner until you have used all the strands up.

f Complete the tree with a **'Time to Stop' Box Stitch** (this is the top of your tree).

g Trim the branches at an angle, all the way around, like this.

h Now make a star with a piece of pipe cleaner for the top of your tree and use the cotton reel as a base. Finally, add baubles using coloured pom poms or small beads.

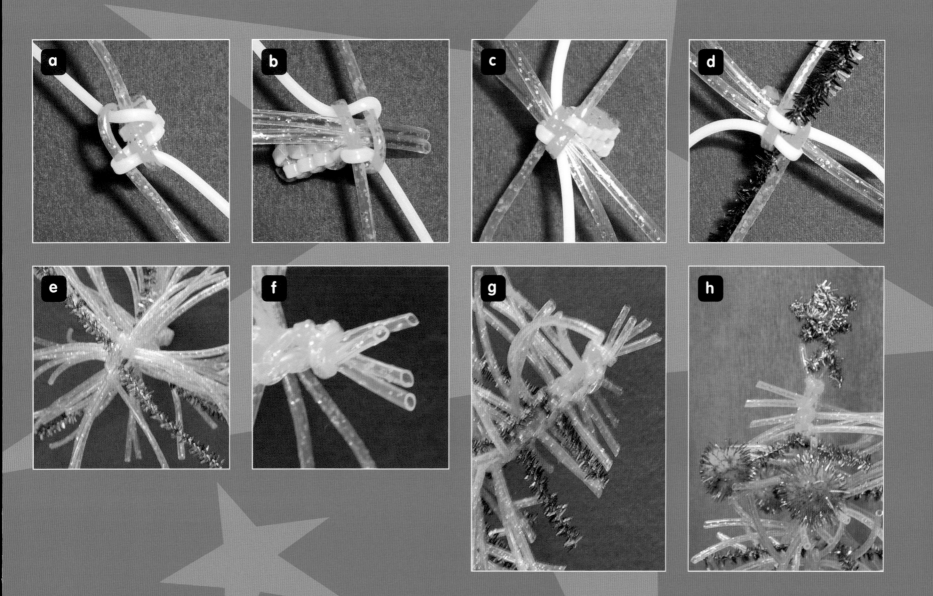

Let's Get Festive!

Bobbing Robin Key-ring

Key-rings can be great stocking-fillers and are really useful too! This key-ring has a seasonal theme to it, and you can use the same basic technique to make all sorts of different birds and animals.

★ You will need: four scoubidou strands, two yellow and two orange, for the legs; one red pom pom for the breast; a small piece of yellow card for the beak; a pair of stick-on eyes; a yellow eraser; a key-ring.

a Make two holes in the eraser about 1cm apart and thread through the two yellow strands. Pull the strands through until the middle of each is located on the hole in the rubber.

b Find the middle of one of the orange strands and create an **'Off We Go' Box Stitch** with one of the yellow strands you have pulled through like this.

c Continue with either **'Moving On' Box Stitch** or **'Moving On' Round & Round Stitch** to make the leg about 6cm long. Cut the ends off 10cm from the end of the project.

d Now you are going to make the foot. Create a **'Moving On' Box Stitch** and leave it loose. Thread two of the short ends through the space you have made to form two small loops.

e Next, feed the other two short ends through the same loosened strand, making two further loops (threading the strands two-at-a-time helps to splay the feet out).

f Pull the loosened stitch tight and cut the end close to the project. You should now have three 'toes'.

g Create the second leg and foot exactly as you did the first, following points **d**, **e** and **f**.

Cut a diamond out of the yellow card, fold in half and stick on as a beak. Stick on the pom pom for the breast and finally, two small eyes.

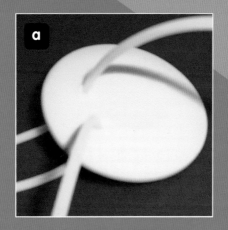

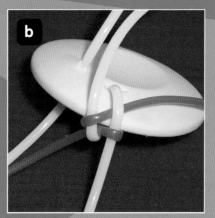

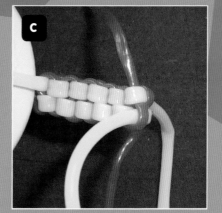

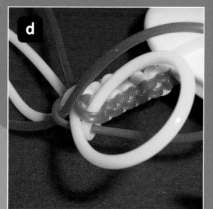

Let's Get Festive!

Licorice Bracelets

Bracelets made from sweets are excellent stocking fillers for mums and sisters. To make sweets into beads you will first need to make a hole in the centre of each big enough to thread a scoubidou strand through and dip them in clear varnish at least three times. This makes the sweets go hard and shiny. Just remember, although they look good enough to eat... they're not!

★ You will need: coloured sweets with holes in and dipped in clear varnish; six scoubidou strands – two black, two white, one blue and one red.

a Knot the six strands together about 10cm from the ends.

b Separate out the strands with the black top and bottom, one white and one colour each side.

c Begin by creating **'Moving On' Over & Under Stitch** to make a pattern like this.

d When you have completed 1cm of this stitch, take one of your sweets and thread it though one of the black strands.

e Create four more **'Moving On' Over & Under Stitches**.

f Now change to **'Moving On' Do the Twist! Stitch**, this creates the diagonal pattern in the finished bracelet. Do six of these stitches.

g Go back to **'Moving On' Over & Under Stitch** for four more stitches and add in another sweet, as you did in point **d**.

h Repeat points **e** to **g** until your bracelet is the length you want.

Finally, trim both ends of the project to about 10cm and tie together like this.

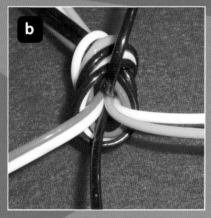

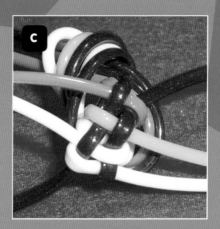

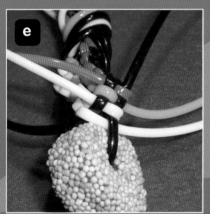

Let's Get Festive!

Crazy Cracker Earrings

We think these earrings are great for Christmas parties. Your friends may think you're completely crackers of course, but where's the harm in that! You can buy earring hooks from craft shops or simply take an old pair apart (as long as you ask permission from a grown-up first).

★ You will need: three scoubidou strands in different, but similar colours for each earring; two small bells or beads for decoration, one sparkly pipe cleaner; two earring hooks.

a Find the centre of the three strands and create an **'Off We Go' Over & Under Stitch**. Continue with **'Moving On' Do the Twist! Stitch** for 1.5cm.

b Wrap a piece of sparkly pipe cleaner around the strands tightly to secure them. Twist the sparkly pipe cleaner together and trim close to the project.

c Now continue again with **'Moving On' Do the Twist! Stitch** for another 1.5cm and thread the bead or bell on to one of the strands. This is the decoration at the centre of the cracker.

d Produce another 1.5cm of **'Moving On' Do the Twist! Stitch**, tie another piece of sparkly pipe cleaner around the strands (as described in point **b**) and finally produce another 1.5cm of **'Moving On' Do the Twist! Stitch**. Finish off the cracker with a **'Time to Stop' Over & Under Stitch**.

e Thread the earring hook through the largest loop in your **'Off We Go' Over & Under Stitch**, making sure the decoration will point to the front when the earring is hung from an ear.

g Finally, follow all the steps from point **a** through to point **e** to make your second earring. Now go out and PARTY!

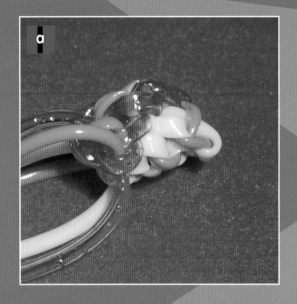

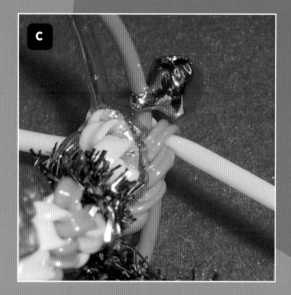

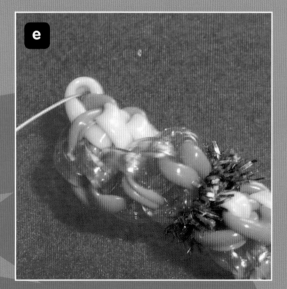

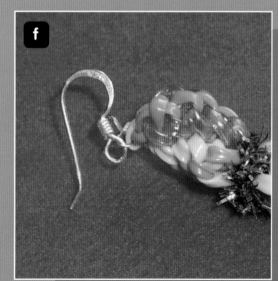

Let's Get Festive!

Rosey Wreaths

Traditional wreaths hung on front doors welcome guests into a festive home. These little wreaths look great hung on door handles and Christmas trees.

★ You will need: twelve scoubidou strands for the wreath in six different colours; one white scoubidou strand for the flowers; two sparkly pipe cleaners; ribbon for decoration.

a Separate the strands into the six different colours. Knot one set of strands together near to the end.

b Work with **'Moving On' Do the Twist! Stitch** using these six strands. You will get a pattern like this.

c Continue until your shortest strand is about 3cm long. Create another **'Moving On' Do the Twist! Stitch**, leaving it loose, and feed about 2cm of the same-colour spare strand through the stitch in the opposite direction. Pull the stitch really tight. Create a new stitch, but this time using the new strand and trim the short ends close to the project.

d Keep working with **'Moving On' Do the Twist! Stitch**, follow the process in **c** as you come to the end of all the other strands. You should

now continue until this second set of strands is about 6cm long (or longer, depending on how large a wreath you want to make). Finish off the stitching with a **'Time to Stop' Over & Under Stitch**. Do not pull this stitch too tight.

e You are now going to join the two ends of the project. Untie the knot at the beginning of the project and loosen the first stitch. Thread strands from each end of the project through the loose stitch in the other end. Every other strand works well. Leave two of the longest strands free.

f Pull the stitches tight and trim off the strands you have pulled through leaving the two longest strands untrimmed. Wrap these loose strands around the join and knot the ends back into this binding to create a neat finish. Trim the ends off.

g Use the two sparkly pipe cleaners to create a loop at the top and spiral around the wreath.

h To make the flowers, tie a loose knot in the white scoubidou strand, looping one end of the strand through this knot several times. Trim the stem to 2cm long and pull through the pipe cleaner spiral. Create four more flowers and add a ribbon.

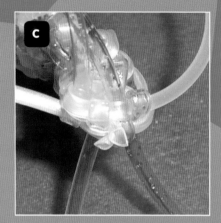

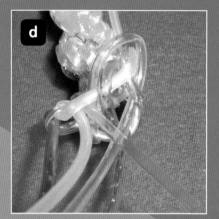

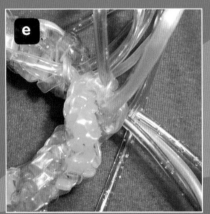

Let's Get Festive!

Reindeer Friends

We couldn't do a Christmas book without these very special Christmassy animals; after all, without them, how would Santa deliver our presents? You will need to be able to do 'Moving On' Over & Under Stitch to make these little reindeer.

★ You will need: four scoubidou strands in oranges and yellows; two red pipe cleaners; a pair of stick-on eyes.

a Find the centre of three of the scoubidou strands and begin with an **'Off We Go' Over & Under Stitch**. Continue with **'Moving On' Over & Under Stitch** for 1.5 cm.

b Using two of the centre strands, tie these across the centre of the project and pull the knot tight. This creates the antlers.

c To make the neck, continue the project with **'Moving On' Box Stitch** using the four remaining strands. Make the neck 1cm long.

d You are now going to make the reindeer's body out of **'Moving On'** **Over & Under Stitch**. To do this, thread the extra strand through the centre of the **'Moving On' Box Stitch** like this.

e Make a body with **'Moving On' Over & Under Stitch**, about 3.5cm long.

f To make the tail, tie two of the centre strands over the other strands pointing upwards and sideways so that all strands are pointing downwards (in the same direction as the head).

g Now make two **'Moving On' Wrap It! Stitches** to secure the tail downwards.

h The antlers are made simply by tieing two knots in each of the free strands on top of the reindeer's head and trimming the ends.

i Choose a matching coloured pipe cleaner to make the legs and cut it in half. Use a bradawl or cocktail stick to stretch the strands out at each end of the body.

j Next, thread the pipe cleaners through and bend to make knees and feet.

k Stick on eyes to complete your reindeer.

… now make him some friends!

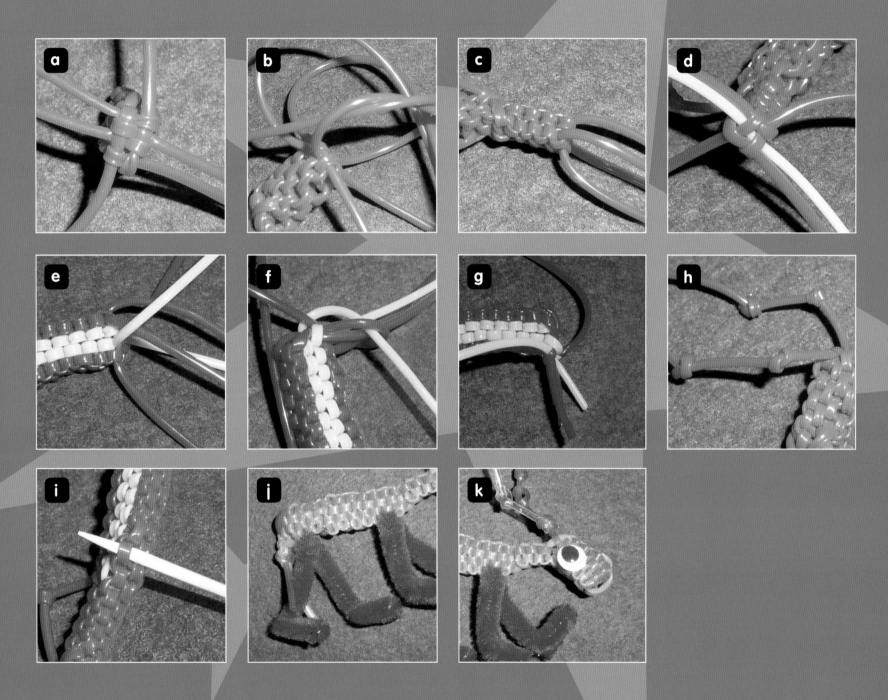

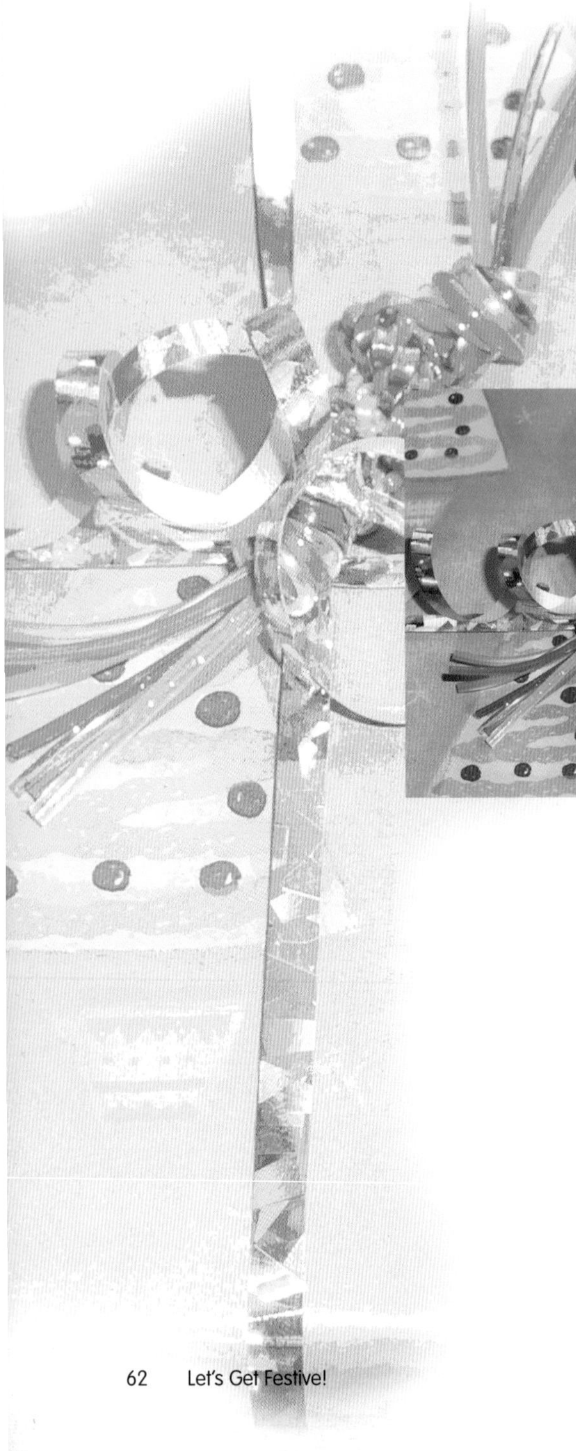

Let's Get Festive!

Parcel Sweets

These parcel decorations are a good challenge for advanced scoubidouers. You will need to be confident with 'Moving On' Do the Twist! Stitch as the technique shown here is an advanced version of this stitch. You can decorate the ends of your sweets with ribbons and bows to make amazing parcels!

★ You will need eight scoubidou strands (the choice of colours is up to you); ribbons to decorate.

a Knot the eight strands together about 4cm from the ends.

b You are now going to create an advanced **'Moving On' Do the Twist! Stitch** with all eight strands. You do this by putting one strand on the left, one on the right, three upwards and three downwards.

Weave the strands exactly as you would for a normal **'Moving On' Do the Twist! Stitch**.

c You will find that you begin to create a deep spiral pattern like this.

d Continue with this stitch for about 3cm, until your spiral has done a full turn.

e Knot this second end and trim all the strands to about 3cm on each side of the sweet.

f You can tie the sweets onto a parcel or simply use as a decoration in a bowl with other sweets you have made in different colours. We have displayed ours with some glass sweets too.

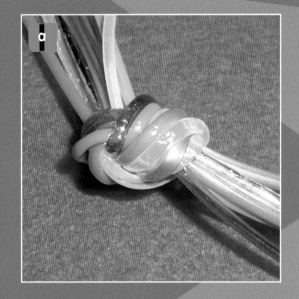

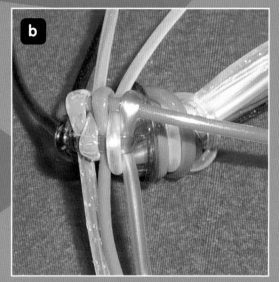

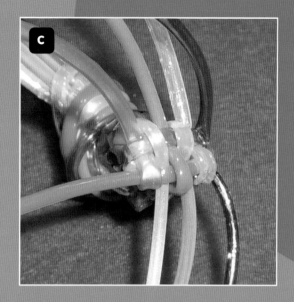

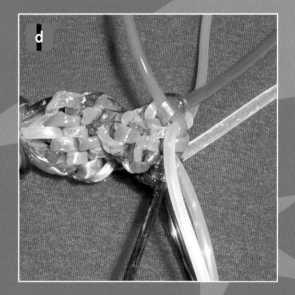

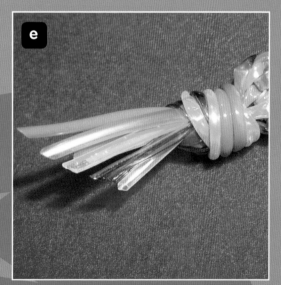

Let's Get Festive!

Baubles!

Now you have been through the book and made some of the projects you are probably full of great ideas to create your own Christmas gifts and decorations.

Baubles are a good place to start and are lots of fun to make. The techniques you have learned will help you to invent many different types and a few ideas are shown here to get you started.

Sparkly pipe cleaners are very useful to bend **Round & Round Stitch** projects into spirals.

Paperclip designs can be combined with other scoubidous to create frames (we have used **Box Stitch** to create the project in the picture).

Try creating your own joins to produce different shapes. Our project shows a triple join with **Round and Round Stitch**, joined together at the base, making a frame for these 'berries'.

A Christmas tree can look really effective if you create a number of baubles in the same design, or a number of designs all in the same colour.

Just remember, think of as many ways as you can to make your projects shine and knot your way to a sparkly scoubidou Christmas!